D0326858

HIP-HOP
MOGULS

An Unauthorized Biography

Kanye West
Hip-Hop Mogul

Jeff Burlingame

Speeding Star
Keep Boys Reading!

Library of Congress Cataloging-in-Publication Data

Burlingame, Jeff.
 Kanye West : hip-hop mogul / Jeff Burlingame.
  pages cm. — (Hip-hop moguls)
 Includes bibliographical references and index.
 Summary: "In this biography of Hip-Hop mogul Kanye West, read about everything from
his childhood and upbringing in Chicago to the birth of his daughter, North West"—Provided
by publisher.
  ISBN 978-1-62285-211-6
  1. West, Kanye—Juvenile literature. 2. Rap musicians—United States—Biography—
Juvenile literature. I. Title.
  ML3930.W42B87 2013
  782.421649092—dc23
  [B]   2013043561

Future Editions:
Paperback ISBN: 978-1-62285-212-3   EPUB ISBN: 978-1-62285-213-0
Single-User PDF ISBN: 978-1-62285-214-7   Multi-User PDF: 978-1-62285-215-4

Printed in the United States of America

052014 Lake Book Manufacturing, Inc., Melrose Park, IL

10 9 8 7 6 5 4 3 2 1

To Our Readers: This book has not been authorized by Kanye West or his agents.

We have done our best to make sure all Internet addresses in this book were active and appropriate
when we went to press. However, the author and the Publisher have no control over, and assume no
liability for, the material available on those Internet sites or on other Web sites they may link to. Any
comments or suggestions can be sent by e-mail to comments@speedingstar.com or to this address:

Speeding Star
Box 398, 40 Industrial Road
Berkeley Heights, NJ 07922
USA
www.speedingstar.com

♻ Enslow Publishers, Inc., is committed to printing our books on recycled paper. The paper in every
book contains 10% to 30% post-consumer waste (PCW). The cover board on the outside of each
book contains 100% PCW. Our goal is to do our part to help young people and the environment too!

Illustration Credits: ©AP Images/Brad Barket, p. 42; ©AP Images/Chad Buchanan, p. 21; ©AP
Images/Damian Dovarganes, pp. 19, 29, 38; ©AP Images/Donald Traill, p. 23; ©AP Images/Eric
Jamison, p. 27; ©AP Images/Jason DeCrow, p. 36; ©AP Images/Jon Super, p. 35; ©AP Images/
Kevork Djansezian, p. 6; ©AP Images/Lynne Sladky, p. 9; ©AP Images/Mark J. Terrill, pp. 10, 40;
©AP Images/Matt Dunham, p. 17; ©AP Images/Matt Sayles, p. 39; ©AP Images/McMullan Co/
Sipa, p. 26; ©AP Images/Paul Beaty, p. 30; ©AP Images/Reed Saxon, pp. 8, 13.

Cover Illustration: ©AP Images/Abdeljalil Bounhar

Contents

Grammy Awards ceremonies are star-studded events. Held at the Staples Center in Los Angeles, they are the American music industry's crowning moment. They are the time when music-business executives, famous celebrities, and excited nominees gather to see who wins the top awards in dozens of categories. Those winners are then called up to the stage to give an acceptance speech.

At the 2005 Grammys, held on February 13, Kanye West was nominated for more awards than any

Chapter 1

Celebrate and Scream

5

other performer. His ten nominations included the coveted Best New Artist award. It was considered one of the biggest of the Grammys, and Kanye believed he deserved to win it. But early in the night, he lost the award for Best New Artist to a band from Los Angeles named Maroon 5, whose singer, Adam Levine, went on to become a judge on the popular television show,

Kanye is shown wearing his angel wings as he performs at the 2005 Grammys.

The Voice. Kanye was angered by the loss. He had a reputation for being a sore loser. A few months earlier at the American Music Awards, he had left abruptly after he lost a similar award. "I definitely was robbed," he told the media after the AMAs. "I was the best new artist this year."

When Kanye lost at the Grammys, even the winning Levine was stunned. "Oh, my God. Kanye West, I want to thank you so much for being unbelievable," he said during Maroon 5's acceptance speech. The loss bothered Kanye for years. In interviews, he often talked about how upset he was over not winning Best New Artist. There was only one chance to win that award. And Kanye missed his.

At the 2005 Grammys, however, Kanye shook off his frustration and did not act out. Many considered that a surprise. But Kanye simply took to the stage to perform his single "Jesus Walks," which was nominated for a couple awards, too. Kanye's performance took place with a church as a backdrop and a gospel choir backing up the suit-and-tie wearing rapper. Kanye was joined on stage by John Legend, Mavis Staples, and the Blind Boys of Alabama. The performance ended with Kanye being lifted in the air, wearing large, white angel wings and surrounded by dancers.

The winner of the Best Rap Album category was announced after Kanye's performance. This was the one category most insiders felt Kanye surely would win. *College Dropout*—Kanye's debut album—had sold more than 2 million copies the previous year, and many critics already had placed it on their lists of the greatest hip-hop albums of all time. The popular *Rolling Stone* magazine had said the album was the best release of 2004. *Spin* magazine did too, saying Kanye "speaks a universal gospel."

After a successful trip to the Grammys, Kanye poses with all three of his Grammy awards.

Kanye "makes it rain."
during a concert.

Kanye was well aware of the praise the album had received and felt certain it would win Best Rap Album. Still, he also knew nothing was certain, and that the National Academy of Recording Arts and Sciences—the body which chooses the Grammy winners—was unpredictable. So when actor Kevin Bacon opened the envelope and read Kanye's name as the winner, the rapper was genuinely surprised. Wearing the white suit he had finished his performance of "Jesus Walks" in

9

and standing off to the side of the stage, Kanye flashed a toothy smile and jogged up the stairs to accept the award. Lifting his hand to silence the cheering crowd, Kanye said: "This is gonna take a while."

Kanye's "a while" turned out to be less than two minutes. But that did not make his speech any less impactful. He began by talking about the car accident he had been in two-and-a-half years earlier that had almost taken his life:

"When I had my accident, I found out at that moment nothing in life is promised except death. If

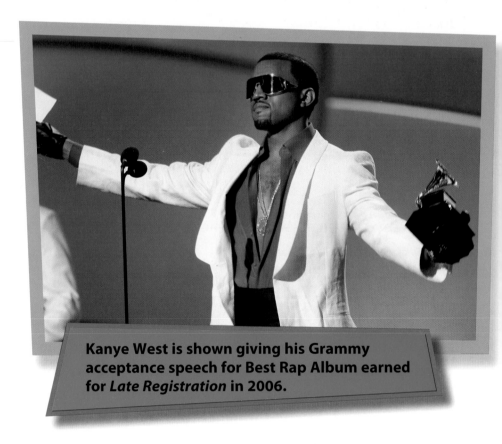

Kanye West is shown giving his Grammy acceptance speech for Best Rap Album earned for *Late Registration* in 2006.

you have the opportunity to play this game of life, you need to appreciate every moment. A lot of people don't appreciate their moment until it's past.…Right now is my time and my moment, thanks to the fans, thanks to the accident, thanks to God.…" Kanye's voice grew louder as he continued:

"I plan to celebrate and scream and pop champagne every chance I get, 'cause I'm at the Grammys, baby! Everybody wanted to know what I would do if I didn't win. I guess we'll never know." Kanye lifted the award above his head and walked off the stage to a standing ovation. The fit many felt Kanye might throw after he lost Best New Artist was not going to happen.

Kanye ended up winning three Grammys in 2005—and has won several more over the course of his career. He's given many acceptance speeches at future awards shows, though none have been as legendary as his first one. Kanye's inspirational speech is one of the most talked-about speeches in the history of awards ceremonies. Through the years, Kanye also has had some not-so-flattering moments at awards ceremonies. He has had a career riddled with controversy, and has created some of the best-selling records in history. He is certainly a polarizing figure: Those who like him *really* like him. Those who dislike him *really* dislike him. And almost everyone knows his name.

Unlike many hip-hop artists, his childhood was not spent hustling inner-city streets. Kanye Omari West was born June 8, 1977, in the Atlanta, Georgia, suburb of Douglasville, to successful parents. His mom, Donda West, was well on her way to earning her doctorate and becoming a university professor. His father, Ray West, worked as a photojournalist and had won many awards for his efforts. The new parents selected the name Kanye [pronounced Con-yay] from a book of African

Chapter 2

Raising Kanye

names because they wanted him to represent his culture. It was an Ethiopian name that meant "the only one." His mom said she chose it because she knew he would be her only child.

Baby Kanye lived with his parents in Atlanta, but shortly after he was born, his parents separated. When Kanye was three years old, they officially divorced. Kanye and his mother then left Atlanta for Chicago, Illinois. Donda West found a good job there teaching

Kanye has always considered his mother one of his best friends.

at Chicago State University. Both parents were active in the civil rights movement, a period of activism where African Americans fought to end racism and bring about equality in the United States and other countries. Ray West was even a member of the Black Panther Party, a sometimes-militant group fighting for equality for all minorities. Donda West raised Kanye by herself during the school year, and he went to stay with his father in Atlanta during spring and summer breaks.

Kanye was raised in Chicago's middle-class South Shore suburb and attended an arts-focused elementary school called John H. Vanderpoel Elementary School. He was considered an intelligent student who occasionally got involved in minor mischief. One day, his mom wrote in her 2007 book *Raising Kanye*, he got into trouble for bringing an adult magazine to school and showing it to the other students. Kanye's mom was embarrassed. "I wanted to crawl through any hole in the floor," she wrote. "…[His teacher] told me that when she asked him where he'd gotten the magazine, he said, 'From my mother's closet.'" Kanye's mother took her son into the car, yelled at him, "…and smacked him across the face." Acting in such a way was out of character for Kanye's mother, who told *Rolling Stone* magazine in 2004 that she "…always worshipped the ground he walked on. People could say I spoiled Kanye. I don't think so. He was very much indulged."

Young Kanye took art lessons and wanted to be a fashion designer when he grew up. By third grade, he had begun rapping lyrics to others' songs. He and his mother traveled a lot. On the way home from one trip to Michigan, five-year-old Kanye wrote a poem in the back seat. "The one line that sticks with me is 'the trees are melting black,'" his mom told *The Chicago Tribune* in 2004. "It was late fall, and the trees had no leaves. He saw how those limbs were etched against the sky, and he described them the way a poet would."

When Kanye was ten years old, his mom was given the opportunity to teach English in China for a year. Kanye went with her. He quickly learned to speak Chinese, and even started a little business for himself where he would charge other kids to watch him break-dance. Kanye was teased by his peers when he returned to the United States. His classmates called him "China Boy." Later, when he was in high school, Kanye also was teased—this time for having big teeth and braces.

By the time Kanye began middle school, his love of music was well known. He entered—and won—all of his school's talent shows. "I would help the others because I just knew I was going to win anyway," he told the *Daily Telegraph* in 2004. "The teachers used to say, 'This ain't meant to be the Kanye West show.'"

During that time, Kanye wrote a rap called "Green Eggs and Ham." His mother took him to a music studio and paid the owner twenty-five dollars to let Kanye record his song. The studio was far from glamorous. It was in someone's basement and the microphone "... was hanging from the ceiling by a wire hanger," Kanye's

mom told *RedEye* in 2004. "But he was so excited, I couldn't say no."

Donda also could not say no to her son's request to buy his first keyboard. When he was fourteen, Kanye used his saved allowance to pay five-hundred dollars for the instrument. From that point on, his mom told *RedEye*, she always knew where to find Kanye. "I never had to worry about 'Where's Kanye?' because he was sitting right there in front of that keyboard." Kanye made and recorded beats with his keyboard. Building on the entrepreneurial spirit he had first shown during his year in China, he began selling those beats to classmates. With the money he made, he bought more musical equipment. Soon, his bedroom looked like a miniature studio. His mom wrote in *Raising Kanye*, "Kanye spent hours mixing, rapping, and writing. It was nonstop.... If anyone, including my dad, wanted to spend time with Kanye, they'd have to go to his room and get in a few words while Kanye made music."

Spending so much time with his music meant something had to give. For Kanye, it was his grades. He went from being an above-average student to one who occasionally would receive Ds and Fs. However, Kanye still excelled in subjects he liked. Art was one of those subjects. Kanye won a college scholarship to the American Academy of Art in Chicago. The scholarship paid for him to attend the school for one semester. He went there for that half-year, then transferred to Chicago State University. Chicago State was a more affordable

While rocking a pair of his "stunna shades" Kanye no longer runs his childhood business of dancing for money, but he does show off his moves during his concerts.

option because his mom worked there. Her employment got Kanye a discount on tuition. But in the end that discount was not enough to keep Kanye in school. He decided he did not need an education to do what he really wanted to do in life. He knew he wanted to make a career in the music industry. So Kanye dropped out of college to pursue his dream.

Years later, it became obvious that Kanye quitting college to pursue a music career proved to be a good move. Immediately after he dropped out, however, the move looked like a terrible one.

Kanye continued living at home with his mother after he quit school. To be allowed to do so, his upset mom said he had to get a job and pay rent. That was his well-educated mother's punishment for him dropping out of college. Kanye was forced to get a job outside of music

Chapter 3

Kanye's Big Break

to pay the bill. He got several, including one as a telemarketer, and met his mom's demands. When he was not working, Kanye continued to use his bedroom as a studio. His friends and musical partners came to the West home at all hours to work and hang out. Eventually this drove his mother crazy. She made a demand: either the music had to go or he did.

His mom's mandate came at a good time for Kanye. He recently had begun earning some serious money off those deep-bassed beats that had rocked his mom's

Kanye might have left school, but he still values education. Here he's performing at Santa Monica High School after teaming up with Musicland to help promote a national giveaway of $150K for a college education.

house for nearly ten years. His first big payday came from Chicago rapper Gravity, aka Grav. Grav paid Kanye eight-thousand dollars for some of his tracks. Years later, Grav recalled the first time he met Kanye and heard his music. He was coming out of a concert, he said, when Kanye ran up to him. Grav had no clue who Kanye was, but Kanye convinced him to come to his car, a compact Nissan, to listen to his music. Grav was impressed and later told media he knew right then that Kanye was a musical prodigy.

Those beats became Kanye's first production credits and ended up on Grav's 1996 album, *Down to Earth*. Kanye's work was featured on several songs on that album, including "Sex," which reached number twenty-nine on *Billboard* magazine's Hot Rap Singles chart. Having a song on the charts was a grand achievement for any person. Kanye accomplished it when he was just nineteen years old. When Kanye quit college, he had told his parents it only would be for a year. If music did not work out in that period of time, he told them, he would return to school. After he sold his music to Grav, he knew returning to school would not be in the cards. "That's when I knew the one-year plan was out the window," he told *Time* magazine in 2005.

Kanye built upon the success of his songs with Grav. Soon, he signed a contract to produce records for Deric "D-Dot" Angelettie. That contract forbid Kanye from releasing his own solo record, which he desperately wanted to do. Because he could not do so, he joined a

Kanye rolls up to the Cannes Film Festival in a $1.7 million Mercedes SLR McLaren Stirling Moss. There were only seventy-five of these made.

Chicago group called the Go-Getters. Kanye was the band's fourth member and its producer. The Go-Getters had some modest local success, and Kanye occasionally was allowed to rap with the group.

Kanye soon moved out of the Chicago apartment he had rented after his mom kicked him out of the house. At that point, he decided he had achieved everything he could in Chicago. So Kanye left for the East Coast and found an apartment in New Jersey, across the water from

New York City. That was the place he felt he needed to be to take the next step in his music career.

Kanye's musical portfolio continued to grow. He produced beats for Ma$e, The Madd Rapper, Trina & Tamara, and other musicians. But none of those jobs were the "big break" he was looking for. At one point, he had almost gotten that break when Columbia Records flirted with offering him a contract. But the label eventually did not make Kanye an offer. The reason, as legend has it, was because Kanye claimed to Columbia executives that he was going to be bigger than Michael Jackson and producer-rapper Jermaine Dupri. Dupri turned out to be the son of one of Columbia's executives with which Kanye was meeting. Columbia never called Kanye back.

Kanye's big break finally came in 2000. That is when he connected with Jay-Z and his record label, Roc-A-Fella Records. Shawn "Jay-Z" Carter already was a superstar by the time he and Kanye met. The Brooklyn, New York, native had released a handful of records on Roc-A-Fella, including *Reasonable Doubt*, which many critics felt was one of the best rap records of all time. Jay-Z was so hot that any musical project he had a hand in "turned to gold."

Kanye's first piece of that gold came when he produced the song "This Can't Be Life," for Jay-Z's album, *The Dynasty: Roc La Familia*. *The Dynasty* became the top-selling album in the United States when it was released. So did the next Jay-Z album, 2001's

After moving to the East Coast, Kanye eventually made his way to New York City where he became close friends with Jay-Z.

groundbreaking *The Blueprint*. Kanye played a much larger role on *The Blueprint* than he had on *The Dynasty*. He produced five songs for *The Blueprint*, including the popular single "Izzo (H.O.V.A)." It was Jay-Z's first top-ten single. The song featured sped-up samples of the Jackson 5's "I Want You Back." Samples—borrowed parts of one artist's songs—were a common device in the hip-hop industry. Sampling was a large part of Kanye's work, too. His tendency was to borrow samples from soul and rhythm and blues artists from the 1960s. He oftentimes would play those samples faster than they were originally recorded, then record them again for use in his material.

Kanye's work with Jay-Z made him a sought-after producer. He produced songs for several Roc-A-Fella rappers as well as many other established, and up-and-coming, rappers, too. Kanye had become the successful musician he had dreamed about becoming since he was a teenager recording beats in his mom's house in Chicago. But Kanye was not satisfied. He had another dream he had not yet met. He wanted to be the one whose name was on the front of the records. He told *Sabotage Times* in 2011, "I never really thought about [just] producing. No one really wanted to produce when I was young.... I was trying to rap. And I made beats because what else was I going to rap on?"

Kanye was making a living off music, but that was not enough for him. Kanye wanted to be the star.

Kanye fought hard to be taken seriously as a rapper. He carried around recordings of his songs wherever he went and played them for anyone he believed could help him become a solo artist. No one would take him seriously. Kanye was thought of as a producer. After several rejections, it seemed as if Kanye might never get the chance to become known as a rapper.

In 2002, Roc-A-Fella finally took a chance on Kanye as a solo artist and signed the twenty-five-year-old to

Chapter 4

Solo Success

Anytime Jay-Z and Kanye work together on a project, the outcome is always a hot track.

a contract. Kanye finally had the shot at his dream. But an incident that occurred that fall threatened to ruin Kanye's chances at superstardom—not to mention his life—before he had hardly begun.

In the early morning of October 23, Kanye crashed his Lexus rental car in Los Angeles. He had just left the recording studio and nearly died in the accident. DJ Whoo Kid, who was with Kanye in the studio that night with rapper Ludacris, said Kanye had sped off from the studio because he was upset with how the evening had went. Kanye ended up in the hospital. His jaw was broken in three places and had to be wired shut for several weeks so it could heal.

Kanye soon turned his near-tragedy into a positive. In a 2011 issue of the *Sabotage Times*, Kanye said: "It gave me the chance to really focus on my music. That was the first time in my career when I could tell people, 'I can't go to the studio with you,' and people weren't trippin'.

Kanye poses with one of his first awards, after winning New Male Artist of the Year at the *Billboard* Music Awards.

Because at that time I was an established producer and everybody wanted me to go to the studio to work on their music, and they didn't' even take it serious when I said I was going to work on mine."

Instead of resting at home to help recover from his injuries, Kanye snuck into the studio to work on finishing his debut record. With few exceptions, most of the songs already had been written. One of those exceptions was a track called "Through the Wire," in which Kanye rapped about his accident, his recovery, and his desire to succeed as a rapper. He recorded his vocals while his jaw was wired shut.

"Through the Wire" was released in September 2003 as the first single off Kanye's forthcoming debut record. The song's video featured footage from his surgical procedures and pictures of a swollen-faced Kanye taken shortly after his accident. The song and the video were well received by critics and by the public. "Through the Wire" found its way into *Billboard*'s top twenty and peaked at number four on the Rap Albums chart.

The song's biggest impact was that it left many people wondering what the rest of Kanye's debut record was going to sound like. That question was answered in February 2004. Kanye's debut—aptly titled *The College Dropout*—was a smash hit. It debuted at number two on *Billboard*'s chart and sold nearly a half-million copies in its first week. Those numbers were comparable to what Jay-Z's records received. By July, *The College Dropout* had sold more than 2 million copies. Critics loved the album, too. *AllMusic* gave it a perfect five-star rating, saying it was "nearly as phenomenal as the boastful West has led everyone to believe.…we were more than aware that West's stature as a producer was undeniable; now we know that he's also a remarkably versatile lyricist and a valuable MC."

In addition to "Through the Wire," *The College Dropout* featured the number one single "Slow Jamz" (with Twista and comedian/actor Jamie Foxx), "All Falls Down," "Jesus Walks," and "The New Workout Plan."

After *The College Dropout* became the hottest album out, Kanye's fan base exploded. He was now one of the top artists in the world.

After forming the Kanye West Foundation, Kanye started raising funds by performing concerts that strictly benefitted the foundation. This picture is from his concert in 2009 at the Chicago Theatre.

Other songs included all-star guest performers. Jay-Z rapped on "Never Let Me Down," Ludacris rapped on "Breathe In Breathe Out," and Talib Kweli and Common traded verses on "Get Em High."

Years later, Kanye told *Sabotage Times* why he felt his first album had been so successful. He said, " … when I came out with *College Dropout* it was weird. It was one of the most hip-hop albums in a while but one of the most pop albums at the same time. So it kind of broke the barrier of people saying that hip-hop wasn't pop, because pop has a negative connotation. But pop just means 'popular'—Michael Jackson was pop."

The College Dropout all but took over Kanye's life for more than a year. He continued to produce for other artists and work on his follow-up album as the accolades for *The College Dropout* piled up. In 2005, Kanye was nominated for ten Grammy Awards, eight for his album and two for his work with singer Alicia Keys. Kanye also was nominated for several more honors—from *Billboard*, MTV, and the NAACP. Many were surprised at the success of Kanye's first album. Kanye was not among them. He already had a reputation of being boastful. The success of *The College Dropout* gave him even more reason to brag. It also allowed him to start his own fashion line, his own record label—G.O.O.D. Music—and the Kanye West Foundation, a charity he began with his mother aimed at helping keep kids in school. Even MTV gave Kanye his own special TV program. It was called *All Eyes on Kanye West*.

Kanye's popularity was so great following the release of *College Dropout* that his hometown of Chicago dedicated an entire day to him. Kanye West Day was held February 27. The star attended a concert at the House of Blues and was given a key to the city by Mayor Richard Daley. The day gave Kanye one more reason to brag. And to be thankful:

"For someone who loves to stunt about how many records he's sold and how much money he's made, I can't believe you guys gave me this to stunt about. You gave me my own day. Lately, I've had to defend myself for being confident all the time, but when something like this happens, you should be able to talk just a little bit. …Three years ago I was standing outside the House of Blues begging to get in, and now I've got Grammys and Mayor Daley giving me the key to the city."

At the beginning of 2006, all eyes were indeed on Kanye. His second album, *Late Registration*, sold twice as many records in its first week as *College Dropout*. Guest stars this time around again included Jay-Z and Jamie Foxx, along with newcomers Brandy, Lupe Fiasco, and Adam Levine of Maroon 5, the band that a year earlier had beaten out Kanye for the Grammy Award for Best New Artist. Singles from the album included "Diamonds from Sierra Leone" and "Gold Digger." "Diamonds"

Chapter 5

Trouble in Paradise

won the Grammy for Best Rap Song, "Gold Digger" won Record of the Year, and *Late Registration* won Best Rap Album.

Kanye's continued success helped feed both his bank account and his ego. On several occasions, that ego got him into trouble. In 2005, for example, Kanye appeared live on television during a fundraiser for the victims of Hurricane Katrina, which killed roughly two thousand people and stranded tens of thousands more when it hit the southeastern United States that August. At the end of his segment, Kanye implied that the president of the United States was racist. "George Bush doesn't care about black people," he said. He later apologized to the president.

The following year, Kanye stormed the stage at the MTV Europe Music Awards after his video for "Touch the Sky" did not win Best Video. The winners of the award went to Justice vs. Simian for their video to the song, "We Are Your Friends." He took the microphone away from the directors of the video who won and explained how he thought the award show lost all credibility because his video did not win. He pulled a similar fit backstage during the 2007 MTV Video Music Awards show in New York after he was nominated for five awards but did not win any.

A similar situation took place two years later during the same awards show at the same venue. This time, country singer Taylor Swift was onstage, accepting the award for Best Female Video for "You Belong With Me."

Kanye's passion sometimes gets the best of him, like during his display at the 2006 MTV Europe Music Awards.

Swift barely had a chance to say thank you before Kanye took to the stage and grabbed the microphone. "Taylor, I'm really happy for you and I'm gonna let you finish," he said, "but Beyoncé had one of the best videos of all time." Kanye was referring to Beyoncé's video for the pop-dance track "Single Ladies (Put a Ring on It)." Later in the show, Beyoncé won Video of the Year and called Swift onstage to finish her acceptance speech. West was criticized for doing what he did. Even President Barack Obama spoke out against Kanye's actions. "The young lady seems like a perfectly nice person, she's getting her award and what's he doing up there?" the president

asked. "He's a jackass." Opinion polls showed a majority of Americans agreed with the president.

Kanye had four albums under his belt by the time the Swift incident took place. In 2007, he had released *Graduation*—which sold just short of one million records during the first week it was available. In 2008, his more-experimental record *808s & Heartbreak* was released. It also sold well. That sustained success had made Kanye one of the most popular performers in America. But the Swift incident knocked him down several notches.

The Taylor Swift incident was one of the lowest points of Kanye's career, and even he realized he was wrong afterwards.

Kanye left the country for a while after he interrupted her, to avoid the harassment he was receiving from the public and from the media.

Kanye apologized to Swift immediately following the incident and continued to apologize when the media asked if he was sorry. He admitted to talk show host Ellen DeGeneres that he had been drinking alcohol and was under a lot of stress at the time. Much of that stress had to do with the death of his mother, whom he frequently said was his best friend. Donda West died in late 2007 from complications from a surgery. She was fifty-eight years old. He wore his emotions for his mother—who had become his manager—on his sleeve. A few days after she died, Kanye broke down in the middle of his show in Paris. When the music for "Hey Mama," a song he wrote about his mom, started playing, Kanye began to cry.

By 2010, the public—or at least his hardcore fans—appeared to have either forgiven or forgotten. That November, Kanye released his fifth album, *My Beautiful Dark Twisted Fantasy.* He had recorded the album in Hawaii, one of the places he had gone following the Taylor Swift incident. *My Beautiful Dark Twisted Fantasy* sold a half-million copies the first week it was on the market. It also debuted as the top album in the United States. It sold well in several other countries, too. The recording featured the singles "Power," "Runaway," "Monster," and "All of the Lights." Critics loved the album, as they had most of Kanye's work. *My Beautiful*

The loss of his mother affected Kanye in so many ways. His mother was not just his mother, but also a great friend and supporter.

Dark Twisted Fantasy won a Grammy Award for Best Rap Album but was not nominated for Album of the Year. Kanye did not act out in public over the snub, as he had in the past. Instead, he blamed himself for the lack of a nomination. He said his next release came out too soon after *My Beautiful Dark Twisted Fantasy*. Kanye believed the hype of his new release had stolen the momentum from *My Beautiful Dark Twisted Fantasy*.

That next release was called *Watch the Throne*. The record was a collaboration between Kanye and his mentor, Jay-Z. It was the first time the two superstars had worked on an entire album together. As with everything the two men touched individually, their collaboration sold well and debuted at number one in the country. Almost every one of the twelve songs was a hit, and seven of them were released as singles. The most successful singles were "Otis," and "Niggas in Paris," a song about Jay-Z and Kanye living the celebrity life in France's capital city. Both "Otis" and "Niggas in Paris" won Grammy Awards.

Kanye's life outside music was nearly as exciting as was his musical life. He continued his involvement in the clothing industry and shoemaker Nike even named a shoe after him. It was called the Air Yeezy. "Yeezy" was

When *Watch the Throne* was released, it instantly became one of the biggest and hottest albums in the world. The tour for the album spanned fifty-seven shows.

Even before Kanye and Kim Kardashian became an official couple in 2012, they had been close friends.

one of Kanye's many nicknames. "The Louis Vuitton Don" and "Ye" were two others. Kanye also had a high-profile endorsement deal with Pepsi and several other companies. He even tried his hand at acting.

Because he was so famous, every move in Kanye's love life was well documented. For years, he dated designer Alexis Phifer. The two were engaged for nearly two years in the mid-2000s but eventually broke it off. He also has been romantically linked to actress Brooke Crittendon, and models Selita Ebanks and Amber Rose. In early 2012, Kanye began dating socialite and reality TV star Kim Kardashian.

Kim Kardashian became pregnant with Kanye's child in late 2012. Their baby was born June 15, 2013. One month earlier, Kardashian had revealed the sex of the baby on her reality TV show, *Keeping Up with the Kardashians*. It was the first child for both the thirty-two-year-old Kardashian and thirty-six-year-old Kanye. They named their baby girl, North West. It seemed 2013 just kept getting better for Kanye. On October 21, 2013, Kim's birthday, Kanye rented out AT&T Park, the home stadium for

Chapter 6

Keeping Up with Kanye

the San Francisco Giants, for their friends and family to celebrate. But the celebration was about to get a lot bigger. After hiring a fifty-person orchestra for the event, Kanye proposed with a ring in the price range of $8 million. After Kim said "Yes," the evening that was originally expected to be a birthday bash, quickly turned into an engagement party for the couple. Kim and Kanye

One thing is for sure with Kanye...he always puts on a good show whenever he steps foot on a stage.

were married on May 24, 2014 in a lavish ceremony in Florence, Italy.

Becoming a father did not slow Kanye's musical career. One month before his daughter was born, his sixth studio album, *Yeezus*, was released. Details of the much-anticipated album were heavily guarded. Little by little, those details were released. When they were released, they were released in grand fashion. In May, for example, Kanye had sixty-six projectors set up in cities across the world. Those projectors showed the video for his song "New Slaves" on the side of buildings. The next day, Kanye performed the song and debuted another, "Black Skinhead," on *Saturday Night Live*.

If the quality of *Yeezus* is anywhere near Kanye's other albums, it is highly likely he will add numerous trophies to his impressive resume. Kanye's three Grammy Awards in 2013 left him with a total of twenty-one for his career. The artist was not at the 2013 ceremony, however. He had instead decided to vacation with Kardashian in Brazil. His absence was not much of a surprise. During a concert a few months prior to the event, he had told fans "...don't expect to see me at the Grammys this year, you know what I mean?" Kanye's main issue was with the Grammy voters. Yes, he had received a lot of awards, he said. But they all had been given in what he considered to be the "black categories." Those were categories— such as Best Rap Album and Best Rap Song—where the nominees were most often African Americans.

Kanye has never shied away from admitting he wants to be known and remembered as one of the greatest musicians of all time, not just one of the best hip-hop artists. He also has admitted that his ego is rather large. In a 2009 episode of VH1's *Storytellers*, Kanye explained why. He said, "I do have an ego and rightfully so. I think people should have an ego. Think about it—I don't offend people, I don't put anyone down. Do I name names or bring people down? That's not my thing. But I give myself big-ups. I feel good about the music I make. God chose me. He made a path for me. I am God's vessel."

Then Kanye revealed that ego: "My greatest pain in life is that I will never be able to see myself perform live."

Discography

The College Dropout, 2004

Late Registration, 2005

Late Orchestration, 2006

Graduation, 2007

808s & Heartbreak, 2008

My Beautiful Dark Twisted Fantasy, 2010

Watch the Throne (with Jay-Z), 2011

Yeezus, 2013

Internet Addresses

OFFICIAL WEBSITE
www.kanyewest.com

OFFICIAL TWITTER PAGE
www.twitter.com/kanyewest

Selected Honors and Awards

2004   Rap Artist of the Year, *Billboard* Music Awards

Male New Artist of the Year, *Billboard* Music Awards

2005   Video of the Year, BET Awards

Best Male Hip-Hop, BET Awards

Best Rap Album, Grammy Awards

Best Rap Song, Grammy Awards

Best R&B Song, Grammy Awards

Best Male Video, MTV Video Music Awards

2006   Best Duet/Collaboration (with Jamie Foxx), BET Awards

Video of the Year (with Jamie Foxx), BET Awards

Best Rap Solo Performance, Grammy Awards

Best Rap Album, Grammy Awards

Best Rap Song, Grammy Awards

2007   Best Hip-Hop Video, BET Awards

Best Live Performance, BET Awards

2008   Best Collaboration (with T-Pain), BET Awards

Best Male Hip-Hop Artist, BET Awards

Best Rap Solo Performance, Grammy Awards

Best Rap Album, Grammy Awards

Best Rap Song, Grammy Awards

Best Rap Performance by a Duo or Group, Grammy Awards

2009 Best Rap/Sung Collaboration, Grammy Awards

Best Rap Performance by a Duo or Group, Grammy Awards

2010 Best Rap Song, Grammy Awards

Best Rap/Sung Collaboration, Grammy Awards

2011 Best Collaboration (with Katy Perry), MTV Video Music Awards

Best Male Hip-Hop Artist, BET Awards

2012 Video of the Year, BET Awards

Best Group (with Jay-Z), BET Awards

Best Rap Song, Grammy Awards

Best Rap Album, Grammy Awards

Best Rap/Sung Collaboration, Grammy Awards

Best Rap Performance, Grammy Awards

2013 Best Rap/Sung Collaboration, Grammy Awards

Best Rap Song, Grammy Awards

Best Rap Performance, Grammy Awards

Index